Kindle Publishing

Work from Home and Generate

Passive Income from Publishing

Kindle eBooks

T. Whitmore

Table of Contents

Introduction

Chapter 1 - How Easy Publishing a Book is Now and Why You Must Take Advantage of It

Chapter 2 - First Concern: What Do I Write?

   For Non-Fiction

   For Fiction

   My Goal is to be a Bestseller!

Chapter 3 – Prepare the Following: Your Title AND Your Keywords

   Your Book Title – Non-Fiction

   Your Book Title – Fiction

   Keywords Are Very Important

Chapter 4 - From Outline to Conclusion: The Twists and Turns of Writing a Book

   Your Outline – Non-Fiction

   Your Outline – Fiction

   Writing THE Book

Chapter 5 - Making Your Pitch (The Description)

Chapter 6 - Your E-book Cover and Formatting Your Book

Chapter 7 - How to Price Your Book and Royalties

Chapter 8 - Promotions and Getting Paid

   Basic but Effective Ways to Promote

   Getting Paid

Chapter 9 - The Pitfalls of Publishing

Chapter 10 - Wrapping Up: The Step by Step Guide in Publishing Your Book on Amazon

Conclusion

Introduction

Ever dreamed of becoming a published author? To see your name written in a book cover; to have people read the words that came from your mind; to establish yourself as an authority.

Now, all these are possible with Kindle Direct Publishing. Kindle Direct Publishing or KDP allows you to publish a book with as little discomfort as possible. Since you've picked this book, it's safe to say that you want to try it out.

Well, you can do more than just try! You can succeed! By having this book, you will:

- Get a clear idea on the things you can write and publish

- Understand the importance of cover, title, and keywords and other factors which can contribute to your success.

- Be organized – from creating the outline to polishing the conclusion. I will also outline some important tools which you can make use of.

- Obtain a general idea on pricing. How can you set a competitive price?

- Have the basic and FREE promotional strategies!

- Learn about the pitfalls of publishing (which beginning authors) do and how you can avoid them

- Discover the step by step guide on publishing your book in KDP

So, if you are ready, let's begin!

Chapter 1 - How Easy Publishing a Book is Now and Why You Must Take Advantage of It

Let's face it: the process of publishing a book has come a long, long way. Traditionally, getting published is equivalent to putting yourself into a ringer: first, there's the trouble of **writing the book to the best of your ability** – if you don't do this, chances are, your work will be rejected not just once, but many times over. You don't want that. So, the challenge is for you to find a good topic (for non-fiction) or a great plot (for fiction). And even though your publisher will take care of proofreading and editing, you must still make certain that your work is not riddled with inaccuracies, grammatical errors, and confusing sentence structures.

After writing a great book, you must then start **finding an agent**. This is another difficult part; you see, finding an agent means you need to categorize your book correctly – is it romance? What kind? New adult? Chick-lit? Paranormal? If it's non-fiction, what's the niche? Is it biographical? Does it concern health? You have to categorize accordingly because literary agents also specialize into specific topics.

Once you have collected the information of your possible agents, you must take care of the **book proposal**, which consists of your complete manuscript (for fiction) or 3 sample chapters with synopsis for each (for non-fiction). Aside from that, you will also prepare the **query letter**, which discusses other details such as target market, an introduction of yourself, synopsis of the entire book, and chapter summaries.

You will send these to the agents you have chosen and proceed to the most excruciating part: **waiting**. Understand this: no matter how much you love your book, there's a chance that it will not be represented by an agent. This doesn't mean that your book is not worth it – maybe you just need to polish your story more or revise your book proposal and query letter.

Perhaps you also need to find more prospective agents. The things that put most authors off are the waiting period and the rejection, but you shouldn't be discouraged! Remember that the world's most renowned authors (like J.K Rowling) got rejected before!

Now, after an agent says "I am willing to represent you." You can say "Hooray!" but only for a little while, because then the agent will send it to the editor for revisions which you might not like. If an offer comes up, then it's time for a little bit of celebration! You will talk royalties, promotions, and publishing. Basically, once a publisher accepts your book, they will take care of everything else and you'll just wait for their instructions, and of course, your earnings.

Remember that all these steps are for just ONE book, unless you have already completed a series and you've submitted it to them all at the same time. If no publisher offers to take your book, the agent (and you) will keep on trying. Should you want to publish another book, you need to undergo the process all over again, but hopefully, it'll be easier since you are already published.

Publishing, the Instant Way

Okay, albeit the subheading is a little exaggerated, it's not entirely untrue. Compared to traditional ways, digital publishing is like a walk in the park. The first part is still present: you need to write a great book. After that, you don't need to find an agent – you just need to keep yourself busy with finding someone who will:

a) proofread your work

b) edit it for you

c) create a set of book covers (2D, 3D or Box Set)

d) format the book

If you already have networks for promotion, then good! But if not, you can also pay someone or a company to take care of the promotion and marketing for you. Request for keyword research, branding, polishing your website, and creating posters or description – all these can be outsourced. Once all the requirements are set, you can just go over to www.kdp.amazon.com to self-publish your digital book – you will also have the option to make it available in print via CreateSpace, another Amazon owned company which handles print-on-demand works. Please note that you need to have an Amazon account before you can publish.

But wait... is Amazon my only choice? Not really. There's Kobo Writing Life, for one, BUT as a beginner, you might want to start with Amazon, since their process is easy, and they have huge number of readers. This book is created exactly for the purpose of helping you write your first book in Amazon. While I cannot promise that your book is going to be a best-seller, since I don't know how YOU will play things out, I guarantee that the contents of this book will be of great help.

A Little Reminder

While this book encourages self-publishing through Amazon's KDP, it doesn't – in any way – declares that self-publishing is better than traditional publishing. I just want to be of help to those people who want to publish their book "instantly" without waiting months or even years to do so.

Alright. Let's now proceed to the first part: deciding what to write about.

Chapter 2 - First Concern: What Do I Write?

That is perhaps the first and the most used question a future author has. Honestly, what are YOU going to write?

For Non-Fiction

If you're leaning on the non-fiction niches, the question can be answered by two questions:

a) What do you WANT to write?

b) What are you KNOWLEDGEABLE about?

The first question will trigger the passionate author in you; you may not be knowledgeable in your chosen topic, but that can be remedied by interviewing and quoting the professionals or experts. Passion or want for the topic is very important because it will show in your book – the readers will be able to sense it. Once they feel it, they will obtain a connection with you.

Knowledge or expertise on the subject is also crucial. Why? It's because readers are looking for experts. For them, buying a book means trusting the author – why would they trust you if you are not an authority on the topic? Let's say you decided to write a book about weight loss: do you think your readers will purchase your book if you have nothing to offer them aside from what you've searched from the internet? They can also surf the net, so why bother with you?

Now, what if you wrote a book about weight loss and the readers saw that you are either one of the following:

- A nutritionist who specializes in planning meals that can increase metabolism

- A weight-loss coach who has success in helping other people attain their ideal weight

- An ordinary man or woman (no certification about weight loss whatsoever) who was able to document your weight loss journey and was successful

I tell you – the readers will appreciate YOU and the chances of them downloading your book are high. They will see you as someone whom they could listen to, because you have experience in your chosen field.

You have BOTH passion and knowledge? Then congratulations! You have even more chances of making it in the Bestseller Section. But wait? Are passion and knowledge my only criteria for choosing a topic? Of course, not! You also have to think about profitability, ease of writing, and the availability of resources (will you be able to interview experts on this topic?). Those two are just the driving forces.

Another question? Yes, I know: ***what if you only have one particular skill or expertise? Does it mean that you can only write one book?*** Not really, unless it is your choice to write one big book. The solution here is to write about a specific topic on your expertise. Let's go back to the weight loss subject – you can write about the following:

- The diet/recipes you used to lose weight
- The exercises you performed – if you used different methods, you can also create separate books
- The little things you did that counted
- The most common problems you encountered and how you overcame them
- The correct mindset that contributed to your success

The point here is, even if you have just one expertise, you can still divide it into several categories, allowing you to write more than just one book. In case you run out of topics, you can expand your knowledge by furthering your studies or skills.

The problem: I don't have any skills or knowledge worthy of being put into a book. Now, to tell you the truth, I doubt that. Every person has an expertise, and I'm not just saying this to flatter you: you may not be certified, or you may not hold a diploma or license, but it doesn't make you any less worthy of getting published if you are knowledgeable enough – which means you have more skills in that field than others who are just beginning.

If you're still in doubt, here's a special post made by All Indie Writers. They enumerated the possible topics which you may have passion or expertise in. Read the entire list here: http://allindiewriters.com/101-niches-to-write-about/, but understand that even at 101, this is still not an exhaustive list.

Writing fiction is like entering a new dimension: you don't know where and how to start. It's like as if whenever you think of a topic, you get the feeling that it's already been made by another and perhaps more successful author. And you don't want that. You don't want readers to write a review that says: "This is story is familiar, but something is missing..." or "I feel like (insert author name) has already written a similar story; well, his/hers is better than this one. I advise you to just read that story since it seems like this one is a second-rate copycat."

Ouch.

Believe me: readers will write these kind of reviews and worse. I have read hundreds of unforgiving reviews which would no doubt hurt the author's feelings, so if you can avoid such a comment, you must do so. Now, I know that thinking of an original plot is HARD. Why? Because there are millions of stories in the market and you HAVEN'T read them all! How could you possibly know that your story is similar to a creation of another author? That's a task which is almost impossible to achieve unless readers inform you of it. Don't worry, I will give you several useful tips in thinking of unique, interesting, and publish-worthy plots:

Tips for Selecting a Fiction Writing Topic

Tip#1 – Think of 3-4 elements that should be present in the story. These elements could be anything! Examples are:

- A hitchhiker, a diary, a meeting with an arrogant man
- A bouquet of flowers, waterfalls, an explosion
- Hearing a piano piece, a blind mother, getting stranded

Think of anything that interests you and cluster them into a group of 3 or 4 (or 5 if you want!)

Tip #2 – Think of an adjective or a set of adjectives that may describe one character in your story. The descriptive words need not to pertain to the protagonist or antagonist – they could also be for the supporting characters.

Tip #3 – Think of one-liners which you want to be present in the book.

Tip #4 – Imagine feeling a very strong emotion. What would it be? Anger? Jealousy? Pity? Joy? What emotions do you want to be in your book?

Tip #5 – Do you have a real event in your life that you want to be featured in your book?

Once you've thought of these things, it will be easier for you to develop a plot because they will trigger your creative juices. The only thing you have to keep in mind is to NOT THINK OF ANY BOOK when thinking of YOUR story. If the topic interests you (or your family members and friends), then there's a high chance that readers will also find it interesting.

My Goal is to be a Bestseller!

If your goal is to be a bestseller, then you must not only write books that you want or books that you are knowledgeable and passionate about. You should also consider the profitability. How do you do that? Simple: you need to do a Market Research.

Market Research isn't about determining what topics are going to sell the most. NO ONE CAN KNOW THAT FOR SURE. It is about knowing that your readers need. It is about understanding what they prefer. If there's a need or a want, then there's a good probability that your book will sell.

So... how do you go about your own market research? Do you need to pay someone to do it? You could, but I won't advise you to. If you want to be in the industry of publishing books for the long haul, you might as well learn to do it yourself. Don't worry, it's not that hard!

Step 1 – Go over to Amazon.com and in the Search Box, proceed to the Kindle Store.

Step 2 – Start typing words like "learn," "improve," and "how to..." If you'll notice, some results will show even without hitting enter. If you type "improve" for example, results like "self-improvement," "improve memory," and "improve your social skills" will show up. It's not alphabetical. Expert authors think that these results are the MOST SEARCHED in Amazon.

If it's most searched, then it means that there's a demand for it. Please don't just stick to the keywords I have given you; you can use others like "income," "flat belly," or "write" – whatever topic you like that comes to your mind.

Step #3 – Click on your preferred result. Let's say you want to write about memory improvement, so you'll click on the "improve memory" result. It will then bring you to the books that have this particular topic.

Now, how do you know that this is a good topic for you? You will look into several criteria:

- In the results, there should be at least one book that's doing a GREAT job; meaning the sales ranking is 10,000 or below. If there's a BESTSELLER, then it's automatic; at least one book is a big player.

- There should also be SOME books that are doing GOOD; meaning their ranks are below 20,000.
- There should be a LOT of books that are doing POORLY; meaning their ranks are below (or above) 100,000.

In the "improve memory" search results, all these criteria are met – however, this still seem like a bad topic to write about. Why? It doesn't satisfy one last requirement which is...

To have at least 50 books, but not more than 200.

At least 50 stipulates that there is enough demand for the topic, but more than 200 suggests that there are A LOT of competition. You will definitely have difficulty in making it big if there already 350-600 book out there with the same topic.

My advice is for you to *be as specific as you could to eliminate competition, but not too specific that you won't be in demand.* For example, why not try "memory palace" instead of "improve memory". If you type that, you'll get around 107 results, but not all of them are about memory palace. There are just around 50-55 books about it.

Why not try it with the topics you have in mind?

Chapter 3 – Prepare the Following: Your Title AND Your Keywords

At this point, I am assuming that you already have a topic in mind. That's good. At least, while reading this chapter, you can apply the principles to your topic. Now, if you are still in the process of deciding on the topic of your book, it's also alright, but you might need to revisit this chapter later on. If you don't want to revisit, you can get a pen and paper and jot down the important points of this section.

Let's start.

Your Book Title – Non-Fiction

A non-fiction book title should be something that would "entice" the readers to buy it. It should be a title that speaks on its own: when the potential reader sees it, he should be able to know right away what's in store for him in case he decides to shell out money to have a copy. Hence, I will present you with the **Rules of Title Creation for Non-Fiction**.

1. Remember the market research you did? As much as possible, **include the words you used in the research for your title**. So, if you've researched about mind palace, might as well have that in the title, so when people search, they will find your book.

2. **Promise the readers something tempting.** Answer this reader question: What can your book give me that other books can't? Think: what will you choose between two titles?

- Photography Business Tips and Tricks
- How to Build a Photography Business in 30 Days or Less!

The first title is too vague, but the second one posits that you CAN start a business within a month, or even less!

3. Be specific: **who is your target audience?** Instead of just saying, The Definitive Guide to Earning Money Online, make it more specific: are you talking about bloggers? Or Forex Traders? Maybe you mean Ebay and Etsy sellers?

4. **Feature the Unique Factor.** Your book should have something unique. For an instance, if many of your competitors talk about *Home Remedies for Thyroid Problems*, why not say: *Herbal Solutions for Thyroidism*.

5. If you have especially quirky personality, **you can play with your title**. Instead of being direct, you can use words that are connected to your main topic. For example: *Chicken Soup for the Soul*. Chicken Soup is known for its soothing

effect for the body, so it will be easy for the readers to understand what the title implies.

One final reminder: you can combine all these techniques or just use one or two, whatever works for your book. However, **make your title as concise as you could**. You want the words to be printed in huge letters so that by only looking at the cover, the readers will have a ballpark idea of what it's about. Hence, don't make long titles or subtitles.

Your Book Title – Fiction

Fiction is very different when it comes to title creation. First of all, you probably won't be allowed to use a subtitle, because really, why would you reveal something in the title when you can do that in the description portion? You cannot be direct, because that would really be awkward: if, for example, your story is about Claire, a housewife who discovered that her husband cheated on her, you cannot use a title like: How Claire Recovered from Infidelity. The title will put the readers off due to two reasons:

- They already know about the story. Infidelity is quite a common topic and seeing that on the topic might make them think of not reading the description at all! That's sad, especially if you have a unique twist in the story.
- It's lame. Why would they read a work of an author who dared to give that sort of title!

While you cannot see a title like that (I really hope you don't!), it gets the point across: **your title should not give away too much information**. It needs to have a mystifying factor enough to make them read your description, or better, read the sample. The more curious they are, the more that they will be excited to have the book.

So then, how should you create your fiction titles? There are several ways around it:

1. Use the Center Piece as your title: It could be the name of the protagonist – *Anna Karenina*, or a description of the protagonist – *The Little Prince* and *My Sister's Keeper by Jodi Picoult*. It could also be the total subject of the story, like *The Davinci Code*.

2. Use the dominating theme, like *Pride and Prejudice*.

3. Use the setting where the story will develop, like *Wuthering Heights*.

4. Use the moment that sets everything into motion, like Linda Howard's *Mr. Perfect*. The title is very appropriate

because things got wild after a group of friends decided to make a list of criteria which would make up the "Perfect Man".

5. Use a paradox, like in *Annie's Song by Catherine Anderson*– Annie, the protagonist is a mute.

6. Use the time or the season when everything was set into motion, like Karen Robard's *One Summer*.

7. Use an important element that summarizes everything in the story, like Emma Darcy's *Last Grand Passion*. Last Grand Passion is the title of the play which the hero wrote; it was about his love for the heroine.

Notice that these titles reveal nothing! You have no choice but to go over the description section to judge them.

Keywords Are Very Important

Once you start the process of publishing your book, you'll notice that you will be asked to include 7 **keywords**. Don't waste them because these keywords are your chance to increase the "visibility" of your book not just in Amazon, but also in the search engines.

A very crucial rule in choosing your keywords is this: **never trick Amazon**. You see, other authors choose keywords like "bestselling" or "on sale" or sometimes even keywords that are connected to a competitor's book – one that sells really well. YOUR KEYWORDS SHOULD BE CONNECTED TO YOUR BOOK'S CONTENT. That's it. Amazon will flag you if they notice that you are trying to trick the system.

Second Rule: Don't use keywords which are already in your title or those that are already dominant in your description.

Also, don't use words that are your categories. Redundancy will not help you.

The idea is for you to use keywords that are also searched in Amazon. So whenever you think of a keyword, test it out in Amazon's search box – just like how we did it in the market research section. You can also use Google's Keyword Tool to help you determine whether that keyword has high or low searches per month.

Aside from the above tips, the best practices here are those recommended by Amazon because they own the system. Here's the link to their guidelines: https://kdp.amazon.com/help?topicId=A2EZES9JAJ6H02

Chapter 4 - From Outline to Conclusion: The Twists and Turns of Writing a Book

You now have your title and the keywords to include in the publishing process. The next big step for you is to write a great book, which, hopefully, will reach the bestseller rank one day. The thing is, before anyone can write a book, he or she must have a clear idea on what to include AND what to remove.

Your Outline – Non-Fiction

In non-fiction book creation, some authors make the mistake of including everything that comes to their mind, not knowing that they are already straying out of their chosen topic! So the first step in writing a book is to create an outline. Don't worry – I have enumerated and explained the steps of outline creation below:

Step #1 – Unleash your thoughts. Sit in front of your computer or get a pen and paper and write down EVERYTHING you want to include in the book. Don't hold back, just write everything. *Hey, but I thought including everything is not a good idea?* Relax; we are just on the first step.

Even when you use a pen and paper, I still advise you to keep your PC open so you can research. Whenever you see something useful, keep the URL of the website. Of course, if you have books, manuals, or reports, it's a good idea to keep track of the important topics and the corresponding pages. It's like creating a table of contents for your research – it will keep things organized, thus saving you time and effort.

Step #2 – Write down your TITLE (and subtitle, if you have one) and analyze which among the topics you listed from Step

#1 are appropriate to include in the book. Don't think about your book being too long or too short – that's not important. The crucial element here is for you to include all the things that SHOULD BE in your work.

Done? Set it aside for now.

Step #3 – Look at all the leftover topics. These are the ideas which you think should not be in the book. You can decide to keep the topics and discuss them in another book, or use them as promotional blog posts. You can also write a report about them and offer it as a bonus.

Step #4 – Take the final list you have from Step #2 and arrange them using the typical outline formula below:

- Introduction

- Chapter 1
- Main Chapters
  - Subtopic 1
  - Subtopic 2
  - Subtopic 3
- Conclusion

Now let's see... what are you going to include in each point?

For the **Introduction**, keep in mind that you want to entice the readers into not just buying the book, but also reading it from start to finish. A good content here is to list down the benefits which the readers will get from your book. Make it as compelling as possible because your intro will most likely be included in Amazon's "Look Inside" feature – a feature that lets readers get a glimpse of the book's beginning.

For **Chapter 1**, you might want to introduce yourself IN CONNECTION to the book. How are things with you *before* you found the things which you will share with the readers? What was the turning point or the moment that you realized things have to change for the better? What were the results of the changes you made? Chapter 1 is establishing a rapport between you and your readers.

For the **Main Chapters**, the points of the topic – which you have in the list – will be discussed. Think: what are the main points? What are the subtopics? It will also help a great deal if you include your references (links and page numbers) below the main chapters.

Conclusion is where you will summarize everything and leave readers with some valuable reminders or encouraging remarks.

Step #5 – Is the most fun of all the steps: you just need to think of appropriate titles. Your chapter titles will be shown in the table of contents, which is included in the "Look Inside" feature, so readers will be able to see it. Make your titles appealing, but not too revealing that readers will be able to just search them on the net. Refer to the examples below:

Bad example:

Chapter 3: 7-Step Guide on How to Build a Professional Author Website

a. Purchasing a domain

b. Choosing a template/theme

c. Deciding on the pages...

      1. The About Page

      2. The Services

See how you have given everything away? Readers will already know the steps and if that's the only thing they are after in your book, they might get the idea that they can just search all the information online!

Good Example:

Chapter 3: 7-Step Guide on How to Build a Professional Author Website

a. Things Most Authors Forget When Purchasing a Domain Name

b. The Best Theme/Template for Your Chosen Niche

c. Constructing the Pages: What's Hot and What's Not?

Notice how the last subtopics were removed so as not to give anything away? And also notice how the new titles are more enticing than the first. Readers will get the feeling that they

NEED to know what you've written because it sounded "intriguing".

Your Outline – Fiction

Now, outline creation for fiction is tough if you DON'T have a clear idea on how the book will progress and how it will end. If you do, then it's probably a bliss unless you decide to change some things midway. Ultimately, everything is up to you: characters, plot, conflict, resolution, scenes, setting, pacing, narration, perspective, and even script! You need to organize your thoughts effectively, hence I will give you some tools which could be useful in your outline creation:

- The traditional way through pen and paper or whiteboard/chalkboard
- Mind Mapping; you can use apps like SimpleMind
- Sticky notes are also a fun way to do your outline

- OneNote and Evernote

- Trello and Scrivener

Choose one that you are most comfortable with, so as not to hinder with your creativity.

Writing THE Book

With your outline ready, it's now time to write a great book. But how do you start? I'll show you the ways:

1. Make a habit out of writing. I don't know about the life you live: you may be a busy mother of 3, a man who's working his way up to the corporate ladder, a businessman in the making, or you could be a retired teacher. You probably have many responsibilities that writing seem like a tough task, but I advise you to set a portion of your day to write. If you're busy, an hour or two is better than waiting and waiting until your schedule is no longer full. If you have more time, try to write for half a day.

2. Track Your Progress. To be more inspired, monitor how you've been doing. You can create a note or an Excel spreadsheet and jot down the following:

- Date and time of the day
- Chapter you've written and word count
- Time it took you to finish

This is also applicable if you're writing a blog post, a freebie book, or a bonus report.

3. Consider Transcription. Most authors think that they can only write by typing, but the truth is, you can speak your book and have it transcribed! There are some free recording tools online; once a recorded audio is made, you have the choice to transcribe it yourself, or have someone transcribe it for you!

4. Write First, Proofread and Edit Later. Focus your attention on writing, and once done, concentrate on proofreading and editing. Don't be conscious of your grammar while writing because it will slow you down.

5. Consider a Ghostwriter. If you are busy and everything you need to complete the book is at your disposal, why not consider hiring a ghostwriter? You will have to monitor his or her work, and remind him or her of your preferred style, but it gets the job done with less worry on your side.

After writing the book, you want to polish it by hiring a proofreader and editor. Online workplaces like Upwork,

Freelance, and Guru have multiple talents – you can pay for their services and stop fretting over an error-riddled book. Another option is Fiverr; there, you will find people who'll edit your book for $5 per 1000 words.

Chapter 5 - Making Your Pitch (The Description)

The book's description is a reader's deciding point: *Will I buy this book... or not?* They will decide to purchase your work if they liked the description, but how do you really come up with an **irresistible** pitch? Here are some tips:

- **Be consistent with your theme** – if your theme is horror, would you write as if your story is romance? No. If the dominant feeling that will set the story in motion is anger, then might as well stir the anger within your readers. The trick is this: get them to feel whatever you want them to feel in connection to the story. For non-fiction books, be sure to sound authoritative, so that readers will trust you.

- **Show the plot/or the features** – Even though you need to mystify the story, you still have to be clear on the plot because that's what the readers are after. It has to be enough – not too little, but not too much.

- **Achievements? Flaunt them a little!** – If you'll notice, some book descriptions begin with the awards the author got; you can do that too, but don't bore the readers with it. Remember that they are interested in your book, not your life. NOTE: Make sure that your achievements are related to your niche.

- **Start with a BANG!** – The first sentence is crucial, so make it as interesting as you could. The first line should hook the readers to finish the entire description, so contemplate on it before making it final.

- **It should be as long as it's supposed to be.** – Nothing more, nothing less. Too long and it gets boring, too short and it gives nothing away.

- **Ask for help at the very end** – And no, I am not telling you to "beg" the readers to buy your book. What you want to do is feature some of the reviews given to you by other readers.

Your description will be posted in all the platforms where your book is available, so take time in constructing it.

Chapter 6 - Your E-book Cover and Formatting Your Book

E-book cover and formatting – these two are often ignored by beginning authors because they become so caught up in writing a great book that they feel like if the plot or content is interesting, as shown in the description, then readers will not hesitate on buying the book.

Wrong principle.

The first thing a person sees when trying to find a good book to read is the cover – not the title, and certainly not the description. Just head over to www.goodreads.com and see how the readers' shelves are arranged: sometimes, they feature the title, at times they only feature the cover. If you visit a book's page, look at the section which says, "Readers Also

Enjoyed". Notice how it only features the book covers. The section which says, "List with this Book" also doesn't include the book titles, only the cover. You have to hover over the image before a title is revealed and you have to click on it before the description becomes available.

Amazon is almost the same, but to be fair, they **almost** always include the book title alongside the book cover. Still though, when a book cover and title are presented in front of you, your eyes will naturally gravitate toward the image because it's more attention-grabbing than mere texts.

My tip for you is to hire someone to do the covers ESPECIALLY if you are not professional graphics designer. **Fiverr.com** is a great starting point; there, you can hire someone to do a professional and unique book cover for only $5. For an additional cost, you can also have the source file, or the version which you can edit. This is a good idea if you feel that your will improve the book in the future. If you want to be adventurous and do the covers by yourself, try **Canva.com**; it's a site where people can create graphics like blog title, Facebook covers, and of course, book covers. They have a pool of images and should you decide to use one, they only cost $1 a piece. **GIMP** is also considered an easy tool to create book covers. You can browse online for simple tutorials. I found a couple of videos on YouTube made by the same person and in my opinion, she explained it really well. Here's a link to the first of her tutorials: https://www.youtube.com/watch?v=WbRxzQdwfHU.

Remember that whatever image you use, it should be copyright free OR you have purchased the rights to do it, otherwise, you risk being sued. If you see an image with watermark, please don't use it! It means the picture should be bought. If you don't want to pay for images, try heading over to **Pixabay.com** – their pictures are mostly in Public Domain, hence you don't need to write any attribution even for commercial use.

For more tips in book cover creation, try reading the following resources:

- http://www.magnoliamedianetwork.com/killer-ebook-cover/
- http://www.writersdigest.com/editor-blogs/there-are-no-rules/general/10-tips-for-effective-book-covers
- http://www.hongkiat.com/blog/designing-book-covers/

For the book's formatting, my advice depends on the type of book you are writing. Is it fiction or non-fiction? If it's non-fiction, I won't advise you to pay someone to format your Kindle book. Why? Because the chance for new editions and updates is high. If you ever decide to make changes in the book, then you might need to hire someone again, causing you to spend more money. If it's fiction, then updates are less likely, so you can hire someone if you really don't have the time to do so.

Do you want to save money? If so, do the formatting yourself. Amazon has published a book which gives you the step-by-step guide, with illustrations. You can download it for free and read it using your browser, Kindle device, or Kindle App. Here's the link for the book: http://www.amazon.com/Building-Your-Kindle-Direct-Publishing-ebook/dp/B007URVZJ6/

Now for books to be made available in print, I'm afraid you have no choice but ask someone to do the formatting UNLESS you are confident that you know how to.

Formatting is very important because readers tend to get annoyed for problems like space, margin, and even bullet points. If they dislike the "appearance" of your book, they might be tempted to return it!

Chapter 7 - How to Price Your Book and Royalties

Pricing your book will make your head spin until you're dizzy. You may have a fair idea on the price of your work, but after a while, doubts will set in. Let's say you decided to price your book at $4.99 – that's fair in your opinion, because of the effort you've poured in writing and the money you spent on proofreading, editing, and cover creation. But after browsing through Amazon, you saw a book that's almost similar to yours and its priced at just $2.99! You read the reviews and noticed that it's good; people already trusted that author, so why would others buy your book when it's more expensive and you have zero testimonials to prove your worth!

You will start thinking: "Hey, if I priced mine lower than $2.99, then maybe people will shift from that book to mine..." But what price will you choose? You only have $1.99 and

$0.99 to choose from and both of these seemed to "devalue" the effort you've poured in!

What now?

My suggestion? Price your book according to the following criteria:

- Think less of production cost (you'll be able to take it back eventually if you have many sales), but more on the "worth" of your book. Try sending copies to beta readers (who are interested in your niche) and ask them how much would they pay for your book.

- Browse similar books and see their average cost.

- Don't be afraid to perform trial and error; Amazon makes it very easy to change the price of your book, so don't hesitate to experiment.

- Remember the royalties: Amazon will only let you get 35% of the sales if you price your book less than $2.99 or greater than $9.99. If you follow that "Amazon Price Box" then you can have 70% of the sales.

- Never lower your price just because of competition. Remember that many people have the "you get what you pay for" idea. So if your book is in $0.99 range, then they might think that it's not as professionally written as those priced at $4.99. Think of your credentials, of the content, and of reviews made by beta readers.

If your book is worth it, then go ahead and price it higher! Soon enough reviews will carry you through and you will be able to crush the competition!

Chapter 8 - Promotions and Getting Paid

Basic but Effective Ways to Promote

What is the goal of promotion? Is it to have lots and lots of sales? Many of you will think so, but the truth is, that's not the MAIN goal. The objective of promotional techniques is to get your book out in the open; to let people know that *hey, my book is live and you might like it, why not take a look?* You see, when you pay for promotion, you don't pay for increased sales – you pay for exposure.

A lot of services are available online which claim they can promote your book to millions of people across the globe, but before you decide to pay them, think about this: how many of these millions of people will really buy your book? If your book is fiction, you might need these millions, but if you are a non-fiction author who specializes in a specific niche, like curing lymphedema, teaching how to garden indoors, or promoting natural beauty, you might not need EVERYONE because not all of them are interested in your niche. You just need a specific group of people to know that your book is up and ready for download.

So where do you promote your book?

- Guest posting in blogs on your niche; try this post which will help you locate niche-specific blog: http://www.crowdfundingpr.org/6-tools-you-can-use-to-find-bloggers-in-your-niche/
- Facebook Groups; search for groups with names like Kindle Books, Book Club, Publishing, and Book Promotion. It'll also help if you seek groups on your niche.
- Send books to websites which offer FREE promotional services:

- https://savvybookwriters.wordpress.com/2012/03/11/18-top-websites-to-promote-your-book-for-free/
- http://www.adweek.com/galleycat/15-places-to-promote-your-book-for-free/77298
- http://kindlepreneur.com/list-sites-promote-free-amazon-books/
- http://www.winchad.com/blog/top-100-websites-for-book-promotion-and-author-promotion

- Ask friends and family to post and tweet your book links.

- Offer contests in Facebook (sharing/liking/commenting) and select random winners who will receive a FREE copy or any freebie related to the book.

- Give copies to top rank reviewers in Amazon and Goodreads. These people have a lot of followers, so take advantage of that.

- Write a free book and offer it for free; in exchange, the recipients of the free copy will give their e-mail address to be a part of your subscriber's list.

Getting Paid

Getting paid in Amazon is quite frustrating because if they do not support your bank, then you have no choice but to choose check as the mode of payment. You also need to reach a certain quota, $100, and wait for two months before they send it to you. For example, if you earned $127 in the month of February, your payment will be sent in April 30th.

Another thing: they don't convert your earnings to USD, so if you earned 37 UK pounds, you need to wait until it reaches 100. They also withhold a certain percentage of your earnings (up to 30%) for tax.

Chapter 9 - The Pitfalls of Publishing

In the author's desire to make it big in the publishing world, they make mistakes. I don't want you to commit them so be vigilant. Take note of the following pitfalls:

- **Creating a blog when you have no time** – If you can't post at least once a week, it means you are busy – don't blog, because readers will feel your inactivity and they won't subscribe to your updates. Lack of time also means less quality. Instead of blogging, why not just share good content using your social media accounts?

- **Offering a free book that's not too good** – people love bonuses! If your free book is bad, then your readers will not buy your next books thinking that the quality is also poor.

- **Hiring a ghostwriter who doesn't care about YOUR book** – bad quality ghostwriters tend to not care about your book, because they only want the payment. The solution here is to pick someone who cares AND monitor their work.

- **Paying someone to review your book** – Just don't. It will backfire if readers notice that many of your reviews are fake. Just let it be. If your book is good, people will take the time to say so.

- **Posing as someone you are not** – Don't invent credentials or invent a person that's not entirely true. Like fake reviews, this deception will also be spotted and it won't help your reputation.

Be honest and stay true to yourself. If you deceive readers, they will look at your book with disdain. And whatever free book or report you give, make sure its high quality.

Chapter 10 - Wrapping Up: The Step by Step Guide in Publishing Your Book on Amazon

Ready to begin? Here is the step by step guide to publish your book on Amazon!

Step #1 – Log in to https://kdp.amazon.com using your Amazon account.

Step #2 – Update your account details; you will be prompted to do this at the top of the page if ever some details are missing.

Step #3 – Finish the Tax Information Interview. This is just a short process where you'll answer the questions in the provided form. Everything is explained in the pages. In the end, you will be asked to provide your Tax Identification Number (from the USA or the country where you are). Based on your answers, your Tax Withholding Rate will be determined. Click here to see the page which offers more information on the Tax Interview.

Once you have finished the above steps, you can proceed on the actual publishing process:

Step #4 – Go to Bookshelf and click on the "Create new title" – it's at the very top of the page.

Step #5 – Enter the book details: Title, Subtitle, Edition Number, Publisher, Description, Contributors (author, editor, etc.), language, and ISBN if you have one; ISBN is not required since Amazon will provide your book's ASIN – Amazon Standard Identification Number.

Step #6 – Choose your publishing rights: is it a public domain work or you own the rights? I'm pretty sure it's the latter.

Step #7 – Fill up the Target Your Audience section. This includes the categories (choose two), age range, grade range, and the 7 keywords.

Step #8 – Select the book release option: are you ready to release it now? Or you want it to be pre-ordered?

Step #9 – Upload the book cover – make sure it's JPEG/JPG or TIF/TIFF and not PNG. More information on cover creation here.

Step #10 – Upload your book. It could be in .DOC, .PDF, or .HTML. For a complete list of accepted formats, click here. While you are at it, choose to either enable or disable DRM. DRM or digital rights management will inhibit unauthorized distribution of the book. Please choose carefully because once the book is published, it couldn't be changed.

Step #11 – Preview your book. Please don't skip this step since you want to see how your book will look like in different devices. If you see a wrong formatting, you can change the content and upload again. You don't have to preview your book on each device – just choose one.

Step #12 – Choose your publishing territories. If you have the complete rights, you can use Worldwide.

Step #13 – Choose your pricing and royalties.

Step #14 – If you have a printed book, you can select Kindle MatchBook, a feature which allows readers to buy Kindle Books at a reduced price if they already bought a printed version from Amazon.

Step #15 – Will you allow lending? Lending is a feature that allows customers to lend the book they purchased to someone else for 14 days. If you chose the 35% royalty, you can disallow the lending feature. If you chose the 70% royalty, you may not.

NOTE: You can choose to enroll your book in KDP Select, but when you do, you cannot publish your book elsewhere for 90 days. The advantages in KDP Select are:

- You can offer the book for FREE for 5 days in the 90-day period OR you can offer it in Kindle Countdown Deal, where the price will increase gradually.

- Amazon customers who enrolled in Prime or Kindle Unlimited can borrow the book. For every 173 pages, Amazon will pay you $1.

Conclusion

Congratulations on finishing this lucrative journey! Before we finally say goodbye, let's have a recap of what we've discussed:

- Niche selection – write topics you are passionate or skilled on.

- Write one topic per book so you could publish another.

- Title creation and keyword search

- Market research

- Creating an outline and writing a great book

- The importance of book covers and formatting

- Simple ways to promote your book

- Basic process of getting paid in Amazon

- The mistakes most author make

- Step by step guide in publishing your book

Be patient; publishing a book will take time and profits will be low at first, but don't be discouraged! Read books and blog posts about publishing for additional knowledge – soon enough, you will be able to build a good reputation.

www.ingramcontent.com/pod-product-compliance
Lightning Source LLC
Chambersburg PA
CBHW060416190526
45169CB00002B/930